How Successful People Manage Their Time and Life

How Successful People Manage Their Time and Life

4 Simple Steps To Declutter Your Mind and Your Schedule

Get more things done in less time with less stress,
and still have time to play.

Jeff Testerman

Contents

ABOUT THE AUTHOR

Jeff Testerman has started 12 businesses in six different states over the past 30 years. He is the father of 12 children, has 18 grandchildren, and has been happily married for 37 years to his high school sweetheart. He writes from his many years of experience and study.

You can contact Jeff Testerman at Dadof12@gmail.com

"Bible Based Businesses—Biblical Principles for Success in Business and Life." (For a limited time you an get this book FREE at **www.Biblebasedbusinesses.com**)

"Every man dies. Not every man really lives."

~ Braveheart

1

IMPORTANT: READ THIS FIRST

Do you feel like you have more things to do than time to do them in?

Are you consistently running behind, never quite finishing a project before you're hit with a half dozen new tasks and obligations?

Jesus said that He came that we may have life and have it abundantly. (John 10:10) Many Christians have life but are not experiencing it abundantly.

This book can help you to remove the roadblocks keeping you from that abundant life.

Can you really experience the transition from burn out to rest, confusion to order, and overwhelm to peace in four simple steps?

Yes! I've experienced it many times. I've watched overwrought widows, CEOs, salesmen, and entrepreneurs go from stress to peace in just a few hours by following these steps.

God's desire is for you to walk in peace and rest. Jesus said, *"Come to me all who are weary and heavy laden and I will give you rest."*

These four simple steps will help you walk in the rest God has for you.

1. Gather—You'll be capturing on paper all the concerns and burdens that are weighing on your mind. *"Let all things be done decently and in order" 1 Corinthians 14:40.*

2. Prioritize and Plan—You'll be sorting and organizing so you can see what you have to work with and which should be done first.

Planning is everything. Develop the habit of planning so you can take action in the most efficient manner.

> *"The plans of the diligent lead surely to plenty, but those of everyone who is hasty, surely to poverty." Proverbs 21:5*

3. Focused Action—Get more done with less stress by learning how to focus.

> *"Let your eyes look straight ahead, and your eyelids look right before you. Ponder the path of your feet, and let all your ways be*

established. Do not turn to the right or the left;" Proverbs 4:25ff

4. Release and Relax. Let go of false expectations and learn to do nothing. You'll discover that sometimes the key to getting more done is doing less.

   "But when they measure themselves by one another and compare themselves with one another, they are not wise." 2 Corinthians 10:12

This book will give you tools to bring your life into order and free you up to live out the dreams God has put in your heart.

You will benefit most from this book by following the steps as you read them. It will bring clarity to what I'm saying.

The first chapters will help you develop the right frame of mind concerning time management and productivity. You must think right to act right.

Then we'll look at the four step process of conquering overwhelm.

Next, we'll look at the big picture of your life, what it is you really want to do by unlocking your passions and dreams.

This is an important step and should not be neglected. It will give you the motivation to press on past difficulties and achieve the success you were meant to achieve.

The last part of the book has some practical help and tips to get you past common time management issues and headaches. You can reference these for reading later when you come across one of these problems.

You will experience some failure in your process of getting this system down. That's okay. Failing will not make you a failure. Even experts who write books on time management get off track and can neglect these simple principles, finding themselves overwhelmed and lost.

When that happens to me I push the reset button, go back to the basics, schedule time to regroup and plan, and get back on the right path.

You don't have to follow this program perfectly for it to work. Good enough is good enough.

"Time is your most precious gift because you only have a set amount of it. You can make more money, but you can't make more time."

~ Rick Warren

2

ADD 25 WORK DAYS TO YOUR YEAR

The Apostle Paul gave us some words of wisdom in his letter to the Ephesus church. *"See that you walk carefully, not in a foolish manner but with wisdom, redeeming the time . . ."*

How are you redeeming your time?

Imagine you are lined up with dozens of other people. Someone goes down the line and gives you all the same amount of money. It doesn't matter your age, race, sex, or position in life, you all get the same amount.

This person tells you that every day you'll be given the same amount of money. You can't save it because at the end of the day it will vaporize forever. However, you can exchange the money for whatever you want.

The things you exchange the money for could be worthless or of great value. It's up to you.

What will you do with your daily gift?

Each day you receive that gift of time. You can spend it how you wish. You can waste time, invest time, or wonder where time went. It comes in the same amount every day, but time is limited. You will have only so much and then it will end.

Time vanishes but the things you exchange time for can last for eternity, be it good or bad.

What do you want to last for eternity?

What memories do you want to create with your time expenditure?

The techniques in this book will save you 49 minutes a day and give you an additional 25 workdays a year to focus on the things you want to do and enjoy doing.

I'm not really bringing anything new and fancy to the table, rather I'm presenting the information in a simple way that will motivate you and enable you to take effective actions to reach your goals and fulfill the desires of your heart.

Who's in control?

Do you control your work or does your work control you? Are you reacting or taking action?

You can manage your life by pain (reactive) or manage for growth (proactive). Pain comes when you feel out of control, when you're not doing what you really want to do. We lose our motivation, passion and fire to face work on a day-to-day basis.

Is this how you want to live your life, missing obligations and opportunities and not keeping promises? Are you tired of feeling guilt, regret, and frustration?

Most people live in the realm of frustration and aimless existence. They wonder, am I missing something? Is this all there is to life?

Walking in peace

There is an alternative to this frustrated wandering.

Picture yourself in a place of peace, contentment and fulfillment. See yourself getting more done in less time and with less stress.

The end of the day comes and you feel energized. You may be physically tired, but your soul is refreshed because you've been getting the most important things done, the things you feel good about doing, the things that ignite your inner fire.

Managing your time instead of time managing you is the key to experiencing this peaceful, fulfilling lifestyle.

Actually, it's not about managing time, it is about managing your activities, your commitments, your projects, and your emotions.

We don't control time—we control our actions. Time is always there. It marches on without stopping day in and day out. We cannot slow it down or speed it up, but we can choose what to insert into time.

You can choose to spend time with your family or work extra hours. You can spend hours surfing the internet or study a course that will improve your sales skills.

It's about action management, not time management.

This is the crux of the matter; the actions you take will produce the fruit of a frustrated lifestyle or a peaceful lifestyle.

Achieving success is simple; it boils down to taking the right actions on a daily basis. If you take the right actions, success will follow. But if you take the wrong actions, things will fall apart.

The actions you take will either help you achieve your dreams or distract you. When we perform actions that align with our dreams, desires and goals, we feel contentment inside, a warm calming feeling.

The actions we choose to take on a daily basis are what form our lives. Our actions determine our quality of life.

This is important to remember: By choosing one action, you automatically exclude another action. It's a choice that we make.

Your ultimate productivity is determined by these choices.

The three W's of productivity: Where, Why, and What.

The best way to be productive is to answer these three questions:

Where am I going?

Why do I want to get there?

What do I need to make the journey?

Answer these questions and you'll be well on your way to productivity.

Where?

With every project you need to ask, "Where am I headed? What is the end result I want to see with this project?" This is also called the goal or the outcome. The clearer the "where," the better the productivity.

The prophet was told by God to write down the vision and make it clear so that he who reads it can run.

Ask where for the big things of life . . ."Where do I want to end up when I take my last breath?"

And ask where for the small things of life, like "Where am I headed today?"

Take this 90-second test. Ask yourself, "Where do I want to be at the end of today? What do I want to have accomplished?" Picture the answer in your mind.

If you do this, you'll feel something shift inside of you. It's a release of energy that gives a boost to your physical body and sharpens your mental clarity.

When I ask the where question, I like to look at time frames of one year, six months, thirty days, weekly and then daily. You can choose what works best for you. Just remember the clearer the where, the better your productivity.

Why?

The why is the energy source, the juice that keeps you on your path to the where.

Setbacks will happen; you'll experience failures and disappointments. If your why isn't strong you'll end up quitting your life's journey and falling into the pit of frustration and futility.

Making money is a weak why. It may take you along the road for a while, but it won't last for the long haul.

You say, "I want to make a million dollars." Why?

You answer, "Because I want to have money." Why?

"So I can help the poor and needy." Why is that important to you?

Keep asking why so you can dig deep to reveal the true motivations.

I encourage you to ask why about everything.

The why is the motivation and inspiration for yourself and for those who work with you. The why will move people to make great sacrifices. Without a strong why you will revert to manipulation instead of inspiration.

If you have a big why for being in business people will be attracted to you because of the why and will buy from you even if your price is higher.

What

The answer to "what" helps you work out the practical day-to-day actions you need to take to reach your where.

What do I need financially to reach my goals?

What do I need in manpower to accomplish my goals?

What knowledge do I need to get this done?

What are the steps I have to take to reach my desired end result?

This book will help you plan your life's journey and answer the where, why, and what of your journey. It will help you manage your actions and time effectively, so you can be more productive.

"Truth is ever to be found in the simplicity, and not in the multiplicity and confusion of things."

~ Isaac Newton

3

STRESS CAUSING, BRAIN NUMBING, PRODUCTIVITY KILLING CLUTTER

Tim, a sales rep, was wondering why he was feeling so stressed out and struggling with depression and frustration. He was always behind on his projects. He felt like he was running, running, running, but getting nowhere.

Then he came across a study from the UCLA's Center on Everyday Lives and Families (CELF). They discovered that clutter has a big impact on our moods and self-esteem.

They found that the more stuff a woman had in her house, the higher the level of cortisol, a stress hormone, was in her system.

He then came across an article at www.psychologytoday. com and learned that clutter "bombards our minds with excessive stimuli . . . causing our senses to work overtime" and "Clutter makes it more difficult to relax, both physically and mentally." " . . . clutter creates feelings of guilt and embarrassment . . ."—"clutter causes frustration . . ."

As Tim looked around his office, he realized that clutter could be adding to his mental and emotional battles and keeping him from being as productive as he could be.

Clutter is a main cause of poor productivity and poor time management. Clear your office space and work areas at home, and clear your mind clutter, and you'll be surprised at how free and happy you'll feel.

Inventory, purge, and organize.

I'm going to show you how to free your mind and your physical spaces of clutter.

Clearing clutter out of your life can open up doors that previously seemed to always be shut. Clearing the clutter from your mind will free you up to dream again.

Getting things on paper will free your mind to focus on the most important things. Our mind is like a computer—if you overload the memory it will freeze up, maybe even crash, and you'll have to reboot.

Always have a notepad sitting close by to catch random thoughts, ideas, and the "Oh, that's right! I need to remember that . . ." thoughts.

Capturing thoughts, ideas, tasks, errands, and anything else on paper will keep your memory clear and uncluttered.

STRESS CAUSING, BRAIN NUMBING, PRODUCTIVITY KILLING CLUTTER

You'll need some file folders, the three tab manila folders.

Be sure to have a pencil, paper, eraser and pen close at hand.

Let's get started!

"Simplicity boils down to two steps: Identify the essential. Eliminate the rest."

~ Leo Babauta

4

GATHER

CLEARING THE CLUTTER FROM YOUR MIND

"Be diligent to know the state of your flocks, and attend to your herds; for riches are not forever." Proverbs 27:23

Here is a simple exhortation encouraging us to know what is going on around us, and it applies to what is inside of us too.

Clutter in our mind interferes with our ability to see clearly. We don't know the state of our finances, career goals or projects because we are overwhelmed and confused.

This chapter will be the first step in getting rid of that confusion.

You're going to take the time to make a list of all the things that weigh on your mind. Write them down on a piece of paper. (You could use an electronic file or software to do this, but for now stick with paper. Your chance to adapt will come later.)

You'll be capturing ideas, obligations, tasks, responsibilities, hopes, projects, and dreams.

As we move through this process, you'll begin to sort the different tasks and projects and start to pinpoint what you really need to work on.

This process will also help you to find those things you really want to work on and devote your time to.

Little by little, you'll be getting a clear picture of what your real purpose and passion are.

Little by little, you'll cast off excess weight and move into the areas you were created to perform in.

Your Catchall list

Get two pieces of paper. They need to have five columns, which you can make by hand or use my simple template at **http://jefftesterman.com/goal-sheets/**

The top of one page will be titled "Career Catchall List" and the other will be titled "Personal Catchall List". Then at the top of two of the columns write "Projects". Here is what it will look like.

Career Catchall List

Projects	Projects			

Begin writing down any activities, ideas, dreams, hopes, responsibilities or burdens that are on your mind.

You'll be using the projects columns to write down projects. A project is any item that involves multiple steps to complete. Writing a book is a project, calling Mary is a task.

In the other columns, you'll be capturing all your other tasks and concerns.

Here are some questions to prompt your thinking.

Career:

What projects are you working on? What projects do you need to work on?

What are the goals you'd like to achieve?

Any articles, books or reports to write?

Upcoming meetings?

Do you have anything to plan like marketing, outreach, events, presentations, or vacations?

Do you want to start a business? Become a CEO? Work from home?

Do you have any equipment to buy or service? People to hire or fire?

Any sales calls to make or phone calls to return?

Is there anything you're waiting on from other people? Write it down.

Picture in your mind the different people you deal with. Are there any commitments or projects you need to do with them?

Any client follow up?

Training you'd like to take?

In your imagination walk through your office or work area.

Do you see anything that is an "Oh, that's right! I need to take care of that" moment?

Personal:

What activities have you committed to that are related to being a parent? A spouse? A friend? A club member? A volunteer?

Do you want to be married?

Do you need to reconnect with aunts, uncles, siblings? Make new friends? Learn communication skills? Plan a special family trip?

Are there chores around the house? Automobile?

Do you need to organize your home office, garage, rooms in your house?

Do you have yard work? Heat and air issues? Household repairs needed? Bicycle? Boat?

In your mind walk through each of your rooms. Do you see anything that you need to take care of?

Do you want to start a diet? Exercise programs? Doctor appointments? Lose weight? Gain weight?

GATHER

Do you want to plan a ski, canoeing, or beach trip? Learn mountain climbing?

What books do you want to read, movies to watch? Exotic vacation to plan? Weddings? Holiday plans?

What's on your mind concerning the spiritual aspect of your life? Books to read? Seminars to attend? Something you need to get in order?

What do you want to be known for? How do you want to serve and encourage others?

Any languages to learn?

Do you have any creative goals? Books to write? Paintings?

Do you want to learn how to dance? Learn to speak in public? Act? Write a song? Learn to speed read?

Any good habits to start or bad habits to break?

Any financial issues? Investment concerns? Asset planning to take care of? Wills? Trusts? How much do you want in savings? Do you want to own a certain car? Buy a boat or RV? Sell a home? Buy a home?

Write down everything that comes to mind even if it seems trivial. It comes to mind because it's on your mind, so get it off your mind and onto paper.

You have just completed your catchall lists.

By writing all this down, you are purging your mind of mental and emotional burdens that have been weighing you down. It's very freeing when you see all the things you have floating around inside your head written down. It brings clarity and lifts a weight off of you. It will free your mind to be more creative.

It's time to take a short five to ten minute break. Get up and stretch, do some exercises, read something fun, watch a short show, or take a walk. Just give your brain a break.

*"Let all things be done decently and in order
. . . For God is not the author of
confusion but of peace."*

1 Corinthians 14:40 and 43

5

PRIORITIZE AND PLAN
PRIORITIZE YOUR CATCHALL LIST

At the end of this process you will have these lists organized and ready to use so you will be more productive and less stressed.

1. Catchall list for career and catchall list for personal

2. Project list for career and project list for personal

3. Current list

4. Calendar (daily list)

Organize your projects

First sort and prioritize your projects.

HOW SUCCESSFUL PEOPLE MANAGE THEIR TIME AND LIFE

I'm going to walk you through a simple process on how to decide what projects to keep, what projects to let go, and what projects to postpone.

Most of us have too many projects going at the same time. Even if we could work 24 hours a day we would still not have enough time to get everything done. You know what that means. You need to do some purging.

You'll be selecting your top five projects and transferring them to your projects list. This is a new piece of paper with the titles "Career Projects" on one and "Personal Projects" on the other. They will have five columns.

Write book	Plan Seminar	Marketing Calendar	Google places	Author page

It will look like this:

This is the easiest way to pick your top five projects.

Read over your project list quickly. Now read it again slowly and ask this question: If you could only do one project this year, which one would you choose?

Write that on your career project sheet and cross it off of your catchall list.

Now with the projects you have left ask the same question: If you could only do one of those projects this year which one would you choose?

Repeat this until you have your top five projects for your career sheet and your top five for your personal sheet.

It is important for now that you stick with only five projects. That is five for career and five for personal.

The main strength of this system is to help you become disciplined in narrowing your choices and purging excess.

The other projects will remain on your catchall list for future reference.

(At the end of this chapter I will give you another way to prioritize your projects. It is not as simple but it is very effective.)

Planning your projects

> *"Productivity is never an accident. It is always the result of a commitment to excellence, intelligent planning, and focused effort."*
> *~ Paul J. Meyer*

Look at your project sheet that has your top five projects written on it.

You'll be using the Where, Why and What of productivity to make your plans. (See Chapter 2 for more information.)

Where: Where are you headed with this project? Where do you want to end up?

Take the time to picture in your mind what the completed project will look like. Be as detailed as possible; use your imagination.

Who will be happy when it's done? What will you feel inside once it's completed? What will it look like? What will it sound like?

Why: Why do you want this project finished? Why is it worth your investment of time? It could be a simple reason or a profound one.

What is the financial, physical and emotional reward you'll receive when it's finished?

What: What action steps need to be taken? What tools do you need? What resources will you need? Whose help do you need?

Write everything you can think of that needs to be done to make the project a success, one action step per line. Write it in the column below your project. Always ask this question: Before I can take this step, what other actions do I need to take? Before I can do that, what do I need to do?

Before you can call Susie, you need to find her number. So now you have two action steps: one is finding the number, and two is calling Susie.

Here is an example of project planning:

Plan Sales Training Seminar

Where: Have a seminar by October 23rd in Dallas.

Why: The increased skills of our sales people will increase the trust of our clients and increase overall profit.

What: Find location

Ask Richard for references as to the best location

Call to confirm location

Settle on date

Call or email Tom to confirm filming

Prepare handouts for printing

Write handouts

Settle on topics

Write email follow-ups

Set up webpage sign up

And so on . . .

At least weekly and often on a daily basis you'll be looking at this project sheet. From your project lists you'll be transferring action steps to your current list. You only transfer tasks that you plan on doing within the next 7-14 days. You'll also be transferring action steps and reminders to your calendar.

I use a manila folder for each project. With this I can keep track of articles, notes or any information related to that project that I want to have for ready reference.

I keep these folders close by for easy access.

Purge and Organize the rest of your list.

As an overview let's look at the lists you have so far. You have a catchall list for your career and your personal life. You have a project list for your career and personal life. There are two more lists you'll be working with; one is a calendar and the other is your "current tasks" list.

Grab your catchall list and look over the items real quick. Which of those items do you need to or want to get done in the next 7-14 days? Write those items on the "Current tasks" list. Download the form at **http://jefftesterman. com/goal-sheets/**

Career Current Tasks

Which of those items need to be scheduled because they are time sensitive?

That would be meetings, calls you have to make on a certain day, appointments, or reports that are due at a certain time. Write them down in your calendar and cross them off your catchall list.

Are there items you're waiting on someone else to do before you can take another step? Make a note in your calendar to follow up with them.

The action steps you write on your "current tasks list" or put in your calendar, need to be crossed off the catchall list.

When you finish this process you will have a list of things that need to be done in the next 7-14 days and items scheduled in your calendar at the appropriate times.

This list, along with your calendar, will be the ones you'll be working from on a daily basis. It will contain mainly your one-action tasks that need to be done soon, your ongoing actions and other reminders, (like checking email, reading over goals, reading a book, prayer time, seminar studies.) You will be looking at your catchall list at least weekly.

Do not put an item on the current list unless you think you're going to work on it within 7-14 days.

Is there a birthday gift you need to buy this week? Write it on your current list or calendar, and cross it off the catchall list.

Is there a financial report due at work this week? Put it on your current list and cross it off your catchall list.

Do you have bills to pay? Put them in your calendar so you won't miss your due dates.

Are you waiting on Alice to get back to you before you schedule the meeting date? Make a note in your calendar about when you need to hear from her.

The tasks and projects left on the catchall list will be your projects, future tasks and maybe-do items. You will review this list weekly.

(I will go into more detail later on how to plan your month, week, and day.)

You should be getting a clear picture of everything that's on your plate and feeling a weight lift off your shoulders as you see things clearly laid out before you.

Some reminders:

The calendar is for tasks that have to be done on a certain day or remembered on a particular day.

The current list is for tasks that you plan to accomplish in the next 7-14 days.

The project list is to track your projects.

The catchall list is for the remaining tasks, projects and future maybe-do items.

If an item stays on the current list and you don't take any action on it, then move it back to the catchall list for a future time.

Daily you'll be adding to your catchall list, calendar and working list. These are the foundations of your system.

Don't trust your memory—use your lists.

Get in the habit of putting everything on one of your lists. If you're out and about and something comes to mind, write it down as soon as you can and when you get back to where your lists are, transfer that to one of the lists.

Tips to think about:

Keep your projects to a minimum. Focus is the key to speed. Trying to do too many projects is counter-productive.

Each month pick one project that you will give special attention to and focus on it. Give it extra time and diligence.

The items you put on your current list come from your project list and catchall list.

Remember, the "why" motivates. It creates emotion and emotion drives action.

The bad news: You will not have time to act on all your projects and ideas. If you try (as you probably have been doing), you'll feel overwhelmed and maybe even a little depressed.

The good news: You don't have to do all your projects. It's okay to say, "No, never", or "No, maybe I'll get to that later".

Wise procrastination or termination of projects can be very freeing. I want you to exercise that right now by looking at your projects and asking some questions.

1. **Are there any projects I can put aside and do in the future or not do at all?**

   There is no greater waste of time than to do something efficiently that does not need to be done at all.

   If so, put a question mark (?) next to them

   I've set projects aside and revisited those three months later only to realize that things have changed and I no longer even want to do them.

2. **What do I really want to do?** What projects make me excited when I think about them?

3. **What projects do I have to do to keep food on the table and clothes on my back?** What projects will add the most to my bottom line financially?

4. **What projects do I have to do to keep the peace?** What have I promised my boss, co-worker, spouse or children I would get done?

   Use these questions as criteria to decide which is the most important project.

Each month you want to focus on this one project. Pour yourself into making progress on it or finishing it. Give yourself permission to neglect other projects (with some exceptions).

You'll be surprised at how much you'll get done when you apply this laser-like focus.

Reevaluate your projects at least monthly to see if priorities have changed.

Now here is a real time saver

Are there any of your projects you can delegate to someone else?

Can you pay someone to complete a project or part of a project?

Don't hesitate to get outside help to make the progress you need to make.

> *"Plans are nothing; planning is everything".*
> Dwight D. Eisenhower

Final notes on projects:

- Prioritize

- Make a planning sheet for each one

- Terminate some

- Postpone some

- Focus on the most important one for 30 days

- Reevaluate and start again

Bonus about prioritizing your projects:

Here is a more complicated but effective way to find your top projects.

Let's say you have 15 projects on this catchall list. Start by comparing project A with project B.

Which project needs to be done first? If you had to choose between the two and you could only do one, which would you choose?

You chose B.

Now compare B with project C. Which project is most important?

You say it's still B, so now you compare B with project D. This time D is more important.

Now you compare D (because it beat out B) with project E. Project D is the higher priority.

Now compare D to F. You realize that F is more important than D.

Keep up this process until you've compared all your projects. After going through all your projects, you've determined that M is your highest priority project.

Write the name of that project in one of the columns.

Now go through the list again and compare the leftover projects using the same process.

This time through you won't be comparing project M because it is already number one.

On this pass, you determine that project C is the top project.

Write the name of that project in one of the columns.

You now have your top two projects in order of priority.

Keep doing this process until you have your top five projects. This should only take five—nine minutes.

Let me repeat what I said earlier. If you're average, you'll have too many projects to complete even if you worked 24 hours a day seven days a week. You must choose to let go of some projects, postpone others, or delegate them to a competent person or group.

"Failing to plan is planning to fail."

~ Alan Lakein

6

HOW TO USE
YOUR LISTS

Here are different ways to use your lists on a day-to-day basis. Several times a day you'll be looking over your lists, so they need to be easily accessible.

First method

Look at your current projects sheets. Are there items on that sheet that you want to move to the current list or calendar? If so, do that now.

Now take your current list and select four items you will focus on today.

Your current list would have items like this:

Read 2C pages in Ultimate Sales

Edit 15 pages in my book

Return bad software

Pay electric bill

File proposals

Work on project _ online training

Call SW about paint problem

Email reminder to Thomas

Study USPS program

Work on project—direct mail 30

Make project sheet for finding personal assistant

Pick four of those items to do today.

In evaluating which tasks to do, use these criteria:

- What contributes most to my highest priority project?

- What tasks will give me peace of mind to complete?

- What tasks contribute most to my financial success?

- Once you pick a task focus on that task; no multi-tasking is allowed.

Some tasks will be ongoing; you won't finish them in a day, like writing a book. What you do is pick an amount of time to spend on that task and consider it done for the day when you've put in your time.

If you finish your four chosen tasks for the day, then go back to your current list and pick another task to do. (And pat yourself on the back.)

If you don't finish all your chosen tasks in a day, evaluate why and learn how to do it better next time.

You can also choose the night before which tasks you must complete the next day. Morning or evening, you decide what works best for you.

Second method

Set a timer for 10 minutes. Pick a task from your current list—any task—and work on it until the timer goes off.

Reset the timer, pick another task, and work on it until the timer goes off.

Do this for 30 to 60 minutes and watch your productivity soar.

You could also use five, seven, or 15-minute intervals.

Third method

Pick a task that you know will take some time to get done. Set the timer for 45 minutes and do nothing else except work on this task. Don't allow any interruptions = no phone calls, no bathroom breaks, nothing except the task.

If you don't finish, then reset the timer and work some more on it or choose another task for 45 minutes, but only after you take a five to 10 minute break.

Fourth method

Use a combination of the above three ways to work your list.

Pick two tasks you know you can get done. When those are finished, set a timer for 10 minutes and work through your list, spending 10 minutes on each task. Do that for 30 to 60 minutes.

Then pick a bigger task, set your timer for 35 minutes and focus on that single task.

If you run out of tasks on your current list then go back to your catchall list and/or projects sheets to pick some more tasks to work on.

What should you do if a task stays on your current list and you keep skipping over it?

Set a timer and work on it for 15 minutes; see if that gets it done or motivates you to work on it later.

If not, transfer the task back to your catchall list with a question mark next to it. Remember, you'll be reviewing your catchall list weekly. If this task still doesn't sit right with you, then cross it off and let it go completely.

Reward yourself

Remember to reward yourself in little ways throughout the day. If you made it through your four tasks then give yourself 30 minutes to read a book, surf the web, or get a special snack.

You could reward yourself after each task with something small and a bigger reward when you finish all of them.

When you complete a big project then celebrate. Go out for a special dinner or a mini vacation.

Rewards are great motivators. Even for adults, they still work, so learn how to tap into them. *"By failing to prepare, you are preparing to fail."*

~ *Benjamin Franklin*

7

PLANNING YOUR MONTH, YOUR WEEK, AND DAY

Now it's time to gather all the pieces together and make a plan for your month, week and day.

> *"A man's heart plans his way, but the LORD directs his path." Proverbs 16:9*

> *"The plans of the diligent lead surely to plenty, but those of everyone who is hasty, surely to poverty." Proverbs 21:5*

Planning is essential but your plans seldom work out as you planned them. Planning is an act of diligence, wisdom and faith. As we are planning our way we make ourselves available so God can order our steps. Our plans are like a sacrifice; we make our plans and then offer them up to God to do with them as He sees fit.

We do our best and surrender that to Him who knows best. We prayerfully and humbly make our plans and then submit to God ordering our steps.

As the above verse says a diligent planner will experience plenty but one who is hasty and acts without planning will lead himself to poverty.

Planning your month first sets the course for you to make progress on the important things in your life. Seeing the big picture will help your planning on a day-to-day basis.

Monthly planning: Once a month one hour

When I make my monthly plan, I do not always fill in all the blanks of week one, week two, week three, and week four mini goals. I do my best but sometimes it can be a challenge.

Planning is a thinking process and thinking is difficult. (That is why so few people do it.)

At the beginning of each month, decide on what will be your highest priority goal for the month. Which project will you focus on?

Every day you will be giving 45 minutes, first thing, to work on this goal.

Now pick two more goals for the month.

Your three monthly goals do not need to be all career oriented. Bring balance to your life.

HOW SUCCESSFUL PEOPLE MANAGE THEIR TIME AND LIFE

Under each week write down some action steps you can take that will get you closer to achieving your goals.

You can find this planning sheet at-
http://jefftesterman.com/goal-sheets/

Monthly goals
1. Book launch (Main focus goal)
2. Exercise program
3. Daily routine

Week one goals
1. Design front and back cover
2. Read bodyweight exercise program
3. Get feedback from editor on layout

Week two goals
1. Set up Twitter announcements
2. Facebook ad designed
3. Make rough outline of daily routine

Week three goals
1. Have Tom start book promotion
2. Schedule Kindle promotional days
3. Design 2 different 5 minute workouts

Week four goals
1. Load book on Kindle and CreateSpace
2. Settle on five daily routine actions
3. Send out Facebook and Twitter announcements

Now you have a good overview of where you'd like to head each month. Don't be afraid to adjust it on the move. Let it be your guide, not your master.

(You will notice at the download page a monthly calendar template that has this monthly planning guide built in to it.)

Weekly planning: Once a week 30 minutes

Friday afternoon, before you leave for the weekend, you need to make a plan for next week. When you do this, you'll find that you sleep better and will enjoy your weekend more.

Each day you will review your catchall list, and see if there are any tasks to move onto the current list.

1. Look at your monthly planning sheet. What actions do you have? Do they still seem appropriate for the upcoming week? Pick three priority actions you're going to take this week that help you make headway towards your goals. Schedule them.

2. Block out time in your calendar for family, fun time, eating, quiet time and down time. Block out that time as if you were writing down an appointment with a client. (30 hours a week)

3. Block out time for your daily morning routine, which may include some of the above items. Allow two hours a day for this. (14 hours a week)

4. Take out your catchall list, current list calendar, and current project folders.

Is there anything on your project sheets or catchall list that needs to be transferred to your current list? If so, do that now.

5. Write into your calendar any firm appointments, meetings, reminders or time-critical tasks that are for next week.

6. Next, block out time to work on your highest priority project. I recommend giving it 45 minutes first thing in the morning, before any interruptions can hit. That will be a total of almost four hours a week (minimum) of devoted, uninterrupted, focused time for working on your main project.

7. Block out time to work on your next highest priority projects. Find two to three hours of time you can commit to your projects each week. It's not three hours each project, but three hours for all the next priority projects. Schedule them just like you would an appointment with a client or your boss.

8. Schedule in your weekly planning time, preferably Friday afternoon or the end of your workweek.

In a week, you have 168 hours to use. So far, you've scheduled time for:

4 hours for highest priority project,
3 hours for your other priority projects,
1 hour for planning,
56 hours sleep,
15 hours for meetings and appointments,

30 hours for family, fun, eating, quiet time,
14 hours daily routine (personal hygiene, exercise, prayer, etc.)

That leaves you with 45 hours of unplanned time. That is almost six eight hour work days.

During your unscheduled times you will scan your current list and decide what you will work on for the next 10 to 45 minutes.

When you find yourself with some free time, do a quick read of your current list. Read it again, but slower, and when something jumps out at you, cross it off the list and then start working on it immediately.

Your schedule could look like this:

Sample Schedule

Monday

5:45 Morning routine

8:00-8:45 Work on highest priority project

9:00-10:15 Work from working list

10:30   Meet with client (Meeting is at 11:00 but I need to allow time to get things together and for travel time)

11:45   Check email

Lunch 12:15-1:00

1:15   Return calls

2:00   Work on next priority project

2:30   Work from working list or deal with interruptions or urgencies

4:00   Meet with Ted about marketing report

4:50   Clear inbox

Tuesday

5:45   Morning routine

8:00-8:45 Work on highest priority project

9:00-10:15 Work from working list

10:30   Watch webinar training

11:30   Check email

Lunch 12:30-1:30

1:40   Call client about next step in the budget agenda

2:00   (or when call is finished) Work from working list

2:30   Return calls and answer emails, if there is time then work from working list

4:00   Meeting with lawyer about wording in new marketing piece

4:30   Clear inbox and work from working list

Wednesday

5:45   Morning routine

8:00-9:20 Breakfast meeting with Tom and Susan

9:45-10:30 Work on highest priority project

10:45   Work from working list

Lunch 12:30-1:30

1:45   Return calls, check email

2:30   Work from working list or deal with interruptions or urgencies

4:00   Work on next highest priority project

4:40   Clear inbox

When you schedule "work from working list" you'll likely have interruptions or "urgent" matters that will arise.

That's all part of working in an imperfect world, being imperfect yourself and having to work with imperfect people.

How to do your daily planning.

Follow the steps I laid out in chapter 6 for working on a day-to-day basis.

When to procrastinate

When new things arise throughout the day and require action the first thing you need to do is postpone acting on them.

If you're on the phone and the person you're talking to wants you to do something, tell them you'll make a note of it and get to it tomorrow or later. You then write it on your current list and get back to what you were working on before the phone call.

Very, very, very, very few things are so urgent that you need to take action on it today. Learn to write things down on your current list and get back to your task at hand, knowing that you can take care of that "false" appearing emergency tomorrow.

Don't let others dictate your schedule. Learn to be proactive, not reactive.

Important note: Most emergencies, if you add a little time and a couple of deep breaths, will take care of themselves or at least be downgraded to a task to be done instead of an urgent requirement.

> *"You do not know the works of God who makes everything. In the morning sow your seed, And*

in the evening do not withhold your hand; For you do not know which will prosper, Either this or that, Or whether both alike will be good." Ecclesiastes 11:6

*"Concentrate all your thoughts upon the work in hand.
The Sun's rays do not burn until brought to a focus."*

~Alexander Graham Bell

8

THE POWER OF FOCUS
THE FALLACY OF MULTITASKING

The third step is focused action not just action but focused action. After you have gathered, prioritized and planned, you need to take massive action.

You decide during planning time but during action time you act. The decisions on what need to be done have already been made. You don't need to think, just act.

Studies have shown that we are not capable of focusing on two things at once. Rene Mariois of the Human Information Processing Laboratory at Vanderbilt University says " . . . Our core limitation is an inability to concentrate on two things at once."

Neuroscientist Earl Miller adds, "People can't multitask very well, and when people say they can, they're deluding themselves." Then he added, "The brain is very good at deluding itself."

The reality is that multitasking is one of the biggest time wasters we face because we have deceived ourselves into believing we can do it when we cannot. (With a 2.5% exception.)

You think you're doing more when in reality you're doing less, and doing poorer quality work.

Multitasking not only keeps us from performing at our best, but it also keeps us from learning and recalling new information.

Some studies done at the University of Michigan revealed that multitasking can make you as much as 40% less effective. Switching from task to task slows you down. The mind needs to warm up for each new task so we lose valuable time when we switch from task to task.

It's like the difference between a car driving down the street without stopping and the mail carrier stopping at each mailbox. Which car will reach the end of the street first?

We may quickly move from one task to another, thinking we're getting a lot done, but in reality we are wasting time.

Close your windows

Control multitasking by closing the extra open windows on your computer. Only have open the programs you'll be using. Computers mimic our brains. The more programs you have open the slower they operate, and if you keep pushing the use of its memory, it will freeze up and crash.

Too many times I've been working on something when an open window distracted me and took me down a path, and I didn't wake up from my stupor for 30 or 40 minutes. Close the windows and get more done faster.

It's time to shut down Twitter, Facebook, texting, and other social distractions. Learn the power of focus and the folly of multitasking.

You need to close all your open windows that are not related to the task at hand, and become focused on getting the thing in front of you done.

Drop the phone.

Don't play with your phone, send texts, read texts or anything else when you're in a meeting or talking with someone. Not only is it rude, but it will cause you to miss important information or have to have information repeated, which is a waste of your time and the other person's time.

If you're on a conference call or listening to someone on the phone, don't be surfing the web or checking your email as it will destroy your ability to concentrate.

How did we survive most of the previous century without cell phones? I think it's crazy how people are attached to their phones, like a baby to its mother with an umbilical cord. You don't have to answer every call that comes in; you have permission to turn it off. Put a voice mail answering message that lets people know that you may not get to their calls for several hours or even longer. I promise you, life will go on.

When you're communicating in person, look people in the eye. Don't continue working on your project while someone is trying to talk to you. Put down what you're doing and look in their eyes. This is a simple yet powerful way to build trust and let people know that they are important to you. The eyes are the gateway into their heart, don't ignore that gate.

Train yourself to focus on whatever is before you.

Tony Robbins said "Most people have no idea of the giant capacity we can immediately command when we focus all of our resources on mastering a single area of our lives."

Whether you are at work or at play, do it with all your strength. Take time off of work to relax and have fun, but you need to focus on your fun. Don't be carrying your work into your play.

Focusing begins with a good plan. (Refer back to the chapter on organizing and prioritizing your projects for help in this area.)

Write out your daily task list, either the night before work or first thing in the morning. Have this list before you so if you feel a distraction coming you can look at your list and get back to what you need to be focused on.

It's easier to stay focused when you have already planned what needs to be done. There is a time to think and a time not to think.

You take time to think in your planning stage, planning your projects, setting goals and planning your dreams.

Don't think . . . work!

On a day-to-day basis, you don't want to think; you want to work. You don't have to think about what you're going to do because you've already thought that through (planning); and now you just act.

Your current list takes away the need for you to think. When you have time to work, look at your working list, pick an action, and act quickly. Move slowly and think when you plan. Move fast when it's time to work.

Let people know that during certain times of the day you are not to be interrupted. This is your focus time. You can accomplish more in two hours with focus than in eight hours of a normal, interruption-filled day.

Imagine the huge increase in productivity if an entire office would block out one to two hours a day where everyone had to focus. No one can interrupt anyone else—no emails, no phone calls, and no breaks. Talk about a competitive advantage!

Use a timer to focus.

Set a timer for 10, 20 or 30 minutes and commit to staying on one task until the timer goes off. When it goes off get up for a two or three minute break, then set the timer and do it again. Train yourself to be able to focus on a given task for 50 minutes.

Don't check email until at least 11 a.m.

One of the fastest ways to get off track is to check email in the morning. It's easy to open up an email, see something that catches your eye, click on a link, and before you know it, you've lost 55 minutes of time doing nothing of value.

Keep your work area clean

Keep your work area clear of everything aside from what you're working on. Loose papers, magazines, or odds and ends will pull your focus away from the project you should be working on.

The 30-day test

Here's a fun trial to do. Pick one project that you will focus on for the next 30 days. It will be the first thing you do every day, and you'll give yourself at least 45 minutes a day of focused time. Push the other projects aside and focus on just this one. Give it a try; you'll be happy with the results.

What should I focus on?

In the next two chapters, you'll find the tools to help you know where you should focus on a day-to-day basis.

"A great leader's courage to fulfill his vision comes from passion, not position."

John Maxwell

9

HOW TO KNOW WHAT YOU REALLY WANT TO DO

I wrestled with where to insert this chapter in the book. Because understanding your passion and seeing your goals clearly is key to living a stress-free productive life.

But I decided to put it here because I felt it was important that you first cleared the clutter from your mind before you could tap into your passions and dreams.

Completing the activities in the next two chapters will help you to place filters in your life that will keep out those deceptive intrusions that try to steal your time and energy.

This process will help you pinpoint what you really want from life. It will clarify your passions and desires and tap into the things that will motivate you to get up each morning with anticipation to face the day.

HOW TO KNOW WHAT YOU REALLY WANT TO DO

Why do we spend so much time doing the things that matter so little to us? Why do we involve ourselves in so many activities that do not help us achieve our goals or fulfill our purpose?

It's because we're unclear as to where we're going, why we should go there, and what values should guide us.

This takes us back to the beginning of book.

"The best way to make the right choices is to know where you're going, know why you want to go there, and know what you need to do to get there."

If you don't know what you want out of life and why you want it, you'll be aimlessly wandering.

Right now, you are working towards a goal.

It's either a goal you've chosen or one that someone else has chosen for you.

Where do you want to go in life? What is your dream? What stirs your heart when you think about doing it? What would you do day in and day out if money was not an issue and you could work at whatever you wanted?

You have to look inside to find this. The Bible says that God gives us the desires of our hearts. What we desire is what He has inspired. When we delight ourselves in Him, then His desires become our desires.

There is hidden within you goals, dreams and plans. You need to do some creative treasure hunting to uncover what God has hidden inside of you.

We were created and formed by the hand of God to fulfill a purpose on earth for His kingdom. It could be anything; a musician, an artist, an entrepreneur, a farmer, a leader in business, a leader in church, a janitor, a mother, a father, a preacher, an explorer, an inventor, a scientist, a doctor, a nurse, a writer, a researcher, an athlete, a politician, and the list goes on and on.

You may be called to make billions of dollars or to reach millions of people, and that's good, but that's no greater than growing a garden and serving only a few. What has your Creator made you for?

Your impact on history and on a society will be measured by the love you have for God and man.

The result is ultimately joy, peace and contentment.

This will look different for different people. Only you know in your heart what is right for you.

Don't let someone else tell you what you need to achieve.

Our society pushes for higher education, diplomas, more money, job security, and preparing for retirement. It's not that they are bad; but what if your calling is different than the norm?

Maybe you don't want to go to college. You might not want to be a homeowner.

My point is that there is no right or wrong; as each person is different. Don't let others (society, parents, friends, enemies, denominations, etc.) put their expectations on you.

Be who you were created to be. complex and international, or simple, quiet and local.

It's time to dream!

What do you want to do with your life? If money was not an issue and someone just gave you 30 million dollars and you were told you had ten years left to live, what would you do? How would you spend your time and money?

Where would you live? What would your career be? Who would you be hanging out with?

Here are some dreams and desires that people have:

- I love hunting/fishing.

- I like to be with my family every day.

- I love the challenge of growing a startup into a successful business.

- I love working with animals.

- I love working in creative arts.

- Training horses is a blast.

- I would love a house on the beach/by a lake/in the woods/downtown New York.

- I want to race dirt bikes.

- I want to make movies that millions of people will come to see.

- I want to be a mother to six children.

- I would love to plant churches across the nation.

- I want to write songs and perform before thousands of people.

- I want to write a book that sets people free from self-condemnation.

- I could teach seminars that help businesses grow and prosper.

- I want to canoe the Mississippi River from north to south.

- I want to discover the cure for cancer.

- I want to become president of the United States.

- I want to travel to all the nations of the world.

- I could work with a group of dynamic people to help orphans in India.

- I want to be a professional football player.

- I want to become a famous actor/actress.

- I could build homes.

- Restoring antique cars is my passion.

- I would have a ranch.

- I am a world-renowned surgeon/journalist/chef/writer etc . . .

- I like to meet new people.

- I like to be left alone and have the privacy to focus on learning.

- I love to have the freedom to manage my own working hours.

- I love to be able to take care of children and the needy.

- I want to live off of five acres.

Now it's your turn. Get alone and dream!

What would you love to be doing? Imagine what your perfect lifestyle would be.

What makes you excited when you think about doing it?

What is it that you do that energizes you even if it's hard work? What makes you feel renewed, pumped up and excited?

What kind of activities do you do that cause you to lose track of time?

What makes you feel good when you do it?

What do you enjoy reading about?

Try to be as specific as possible and avoid generalities.

Write down all the things you dream about doing, have an excitement for or have a passion to act on. Don't hold back. Make a list.

Major Roadblock

Religious people can have a hard time here. Somehow, we feel it's wrong to really enjoy something outside of reading the Bible or going to church.

If you don't have at least one dream on your list that you'd be embarrassed to read in front of a Sunday school class, it's because you're suppressing your dreams and passions. Don't let false expectations or standards keep you from tapping into the desires of your heart.

If you've been born again, you've received a new heart and a new mind. You have the mind of Christ and the Spirit of God living in you. No longer are you the unregenerate person caught up with the lusts of the world. You have been recreated with a new heart, spirit, and mind, that are lined up with God's kingdom.

The desires of your heart have been placed there by God. Yes, your passions can be abused and get out of control, but that does not mean they're wrong.

You can bring your passions under the covering of your values, morals and belief system. However, don't pour water on the fire of your passions.

Write down your dreams, passions, and want to do items.

Finding your top five passions

You should have a list of seven to 15 things you really want to do. We're going to find out which one is your top passion.

Go to your list and start with your first two passions listed. Compare one with two and ask yourself, which one feels better to you? Which one comes out on top? Which one burns in your heart more than the other? Which one gets your heart beating faster than the other?

Go with your gut level feelings. Do not overthink; do this quickly.

If number two wins out, then compare number two with number three. Which one comes out on top? Which one burns in your heart more than the other? Which one gets your heart beating faster than the other?

If number two still wins then compare two with four. Which one comes out on top? Which one burns in your heart more than the other? Which one gets your heart beating faster than the other?

If you go through your whole list and number two is still the winner then circle it. Now you know your top passion/ dream.

Now start all over again. Compare number one with number three. (You will not be comparing number two anymore). Which one comes out on top? Which one burns in your heart more than the other? Which one gets your heart beating faster than the other?

If number three wins over number one then compare three with four. Which one comes out on top? Which one burns in your heart more than the other? Which one gets your heart beating faster than the other?

If number three wins again then compare three with five. Which one comes out on top? Which one burns in your heart more than the other? Which one gets your heart beating faster than the other?

If number five wins then compare five with six. Which one comes out on top? Which one burns in your heart more than the other? Which one gets your heart beating faster than the other?

Continue with the winner until you reach the end of the list. For example, let's say five wins until you reach number 12, then 12 comes out on top. Now you compare 12 with 13 and so on. If 12 ends up trumping 14 and 15, then 12 has become your second top passion.

Keep doing this until you have your top five passions. This should only take about five minutes or less.

This might be hard to follow by reading it, so here is a link of this in action. Lance Wallnau does an excellent job with this whole process.

http://sevenmu.kajabi.com/ fe/22405-step-2-passion-vs-values

This is the beginning. The first time you do this, you will gain exciting clarity about your passions.

Don't do it just once; revisit this in a month and you might be surprised at the new discoveries you find.

How it works together

Going through this process helps you to unlock the true purpose and passions of your life.

Now you can weigh all your projects and goals against your passions. Are your day-to-day activities in alignment with your purpose and passions?

For most people the answer is no. And that's okay for now. Your goal is to walk in your purpose and passion on a daily basis.

For now, you'll be making small steps day—in and day—out to get you to that place.

This is not an overnight accomplishment. It's a process that involves challenges, failures, victories, learning, and persistence. Embrace the process. It's what prepares you to fully walk in your dreams and passions.

Now I'm going to ask you to do one more thing. This will help you clarify everything you just did with your passions and dreams.

Don't skip this step

Take your top five passions and weave them into a story about your ideal life. Write the story with as much emotion and feeling as you possibly can.

We do not do anything until our emotions are touched. The emotional part of us is what moves us and motivates us. This life story is a powerful tool to stir your emotions and keep you focused on what you really want out of life.

You can also include your six goals in this life story.

Here is a sample of a life story:

> *I wake up in the morning refreshed, rested and ready to go. I start out with 10 minutes of stretching and exercises. I step on the scales and see that I'm at 185lbs. I spend the next hour going through my prayer list and reading the Word.*

I'm sitting on our screened-in wrap-around porch that surrounds our four-bedroom home with a large in-ground pool.

I eat a healthy breakfast with my wife and then go to my state-of-the-art office, with a stand up desk, plenty of room, an up-to-date printer, and computers. The walls are lined with bookshelves and books.

I spend time researching, writing, and putting together presentations. I film a couple of five-minute videos to put online. I contact my crew of outsourcers and make sure everything is on track.

Online I notice that my bank account shows $1,129,345 dollars in the savings account and $234,897 in the checking account. I write a check out to Unreached Villages for $75,000 to provide for three van teams for a year.

At 11 a.m. my wife and I are heading to the port in our 2-year-old, blue Toyota Avalon, where we will get on a cruise ship. I'll be doing a seven-day seminar, and my wife will be doing some teaching too.

I brought my guitar because I knew I'd have free time to play.

Write out your dream lifestyle now.

HOW SUCCESSFUL PEOPLE MANAGE THEIR TIME AND LIFE

Read this weekly during your planning time. Let it percolate in your soul and spirit.

"You are never too old to set another goal or to dream a new dream."
C. S. Lewis

"Setting goals is the first step in turning the invisible into the visible."

~Tony Robbins

10

THE PRACTICALITY OF GOALS

A goal is something you want to accomplish, achieve, or get done. It's a target you're aiming for.

Goals are the stepping-stones to reaching a lifestyle where you are living out your passions.

Every day you're reaching goals such as:

"I need to get to work on time today." That's a goal.

"I want to eat lunch and dinner today." That's a mini—goal.

Each of the projects you listed is a major goal with several mini-goals. You have big goals and small goals. One goal may take over a year to complete, while another goal may be to call George today.

Goals fall into these categories:

1. Dreams to accomplish. (long-range goals)

2. Projects to get done so you can fulfill your dreams. (short to mid-term goals)

3. Actions to take so you can accomplish your projects. (daily, weekly goals)

You should have goals in each area of your life to experience alignment and fulfillment.

What you did earlier in this book was to clear your mind so you can think clearly and stay on top of current responsibilities.

Right now you're going to set goals in areas you want to make changes in.

You're becoming proactive rather than reactive.

Here are the key areas of your life.

Personal growth: What are bad habits you want to break or good habits you want to establish? What do you want to learn so you can improve yourself emotionally or mentally?

Spiritual: What is your relationship to God and His people. How can you get closer and more intimate with your Creator? What do you want to see accomplished in this area?

Relationship: Concerning your family, siblings, wife or husband, parents, friends, co-workers, etc., what do you want to see accomplished in this area?

Career: What do you need to advance your career or change careers? How could you grow and improve your business? What do you want to see accomplished in this area?

Financial: How much money do you want in savings? Do you have a retirement plan? What physical assets do you want to acquire? What do you want to see accomplished in this area?

Health: This is the physical condition, food you eat, weight control. What do you want to see accomplished in this area?

You'll be writing down the things you'd like to accomplish in each of those areas.

Clarity is the key to change, you need to know where you're going.

Most people don't receive what they want, because most people don't know what they want. In reality most people are getting what they want, which is little or nothing.

> *"Where there is no vision the people perish."*
> *Proverbs 29:18*

If you don't know clearly where you are going then you are going nowhere fast, and you will arrive there sooner rather than later.

Ask yourself some questions:

What do you want to see accomplished in each area of your life? What problems do you want solved in your life? These are things personal to you. They are not obligations.

Take 20 to 30 minutes to do a fast brainstorm in each of the life areas: financial, relationships, spiritual, career, health, and personal growth. Get a piece of paper for each area, and start writing fast. What do you want to accomplish, change or achieve in each area? You can use this goal sheet if you want to.

Goal sheet 1

Personal goals	Spiritual goals	Relationship goals
Career goals	Financial goals	Health goals

You can also get the goal sheets at www.JeffTesterman.com/goalsheets

Some areas may have a dozen goals; some may have only one. Some goals may be grandiose, and some may be as simple as "call Mom once a week."

Listen don't get hung up on the details of goal setting; Just pick a target. Don't worry about putting a date on a goal. Just start writing.

Here are some ideas of what various goals might look like.

Personal growth:

I want to know the history of the Civil War and its major battles.

I want to learn French by July of 2015 for my Europe trip.

I want to stop chewing my fingernails.

I want to set in place a daily routine.

I want to take a cruise in the Mediterranean Sea.

Spiritual:

I will have read the book *"Treasure Hunt"*.

I will read and pray every morning for 25 minutes.

I will teach a class at church.

Relationships:

I will take my wife dancing at least two times a month.

The family will go camping this summer.

We will take a grandchild out to lunch every other week.

I will read the book *"Love and Respect"* and discuss it with my wife.

I will hang out with my friends and do something fun twice a month.

Career:

I will finish my book.

I will find a manager for my business.

I will go back to school to learn a new trade.

I will set up systems in each area of my business.

Financial:

I will have 450,000 dollars in my IRA account.

My house will be paid off by_____.

I want to buy a new motorcycle.

Health:

I will do 50 pushups, 150 squats, and 15 pull-ups.

I will eat from a healthy menu I put together.

I want my body fat down to 15%.

Pick one goal in each area.

Now it's time to narrow down your goals to one per area.

Don't stress over this; one goal is as good as another. Just pick one. Write it on goal sheet two under the appropriate heading.

Under each of your life areas, you probably have several goals written down. Pick one goal from each area. One from personal growth, one from spiritual, one from health, and so on.

If you could only reach one goal from that area of your life, which would you choose?

If you're struggling with which goal to pick then flip a coin. You'll end up being happy with whatever you choose.

You can also get the goal sheets at: www.JeffTesterman.com/goalsheets

Goal Sheet 2. One goal per area.

Personal goal	Spiritual goal	Relationship goal
Why	Why	Why
What	What	What
Career goal	Financial goal	Health goal
Why	Why	Why
What	What	What

You've picked one goal for each area. This is what we call the "where"; it is your destination. Use your imagination to clearly see the end result, feel it, hear it, smell it, and feel the emotion of it.

Next, under each goal write the why.

Why: This is the motivator. You will not get far if you don't have an important why. Why do you want to reach this goal? How will it make you feel? Will it relieve pressure and stress? The why can help you align your values with your passions and day-to-day actions.

"Why" is the emotion that will press you through the challenges that will come your way. "Why" is the fuel of goal achievement and effective time management.

What: What do I need to reach this goal?

Now write three to five things you need to do to reach your goals. You can add to this later, but for now just put three to five things down. This is the what.

This is the practical get it done question. How much money will you need? What resources will you have to have to get this accomplished? Whose help do you need? What skills and talents are needed?

Don't try to do too much; focus on taking little steps.

Use your imagination and picture the end result you want with each goal. Take the time to imagine how you'll feel when you've reached your goal.

Why am I hammering this home so much? Because you need clarity in where you want to go and why you want to get there in order to have any effectiveness with time management.

Planning can be difficult. You have to think and think hard, but planning saves you time. Once you know where you really want to go and what you need to do, then you can say no to the multitude of other things that are thrown at you from people all around you.

You can say no because you have a clear yes.

You now have six goals for your life.

You need to read these goals daily.

Pick one goal a month to focus on and devote at least 45 minutes each day to taking some form of action that will make progress towards that goal. You could read a book, attend a seminar, or take time to plan and think.

For one month, focus on one goal. If you do this every month and rotate your goals, you will have made tremendous progress toward all six goals in a year's time.

Take one step each day towards one of your goals. You can do more if you want to, but focus on taking one step.

This is a marathon, not a sprint. Take little, steady, persistent steps. Don't worry about finishing fast. Don't set a timetable.

Remember—slow, steady, persistent."*Eliminate physical clutter.*

More importantly, eliminate spiritual clutter."

~D.H. Mondfleur

11

CLEAR YOUR DESK AND WORKSPACE

Now it's time to clear your desk. Set aside a nice block of time, this is important; schedule yourself about two hours of free time, no interruptions allowed, so you can get your desk in order.

This is where you will need a trash bag, box and file folders.

Every extra item on your desk is a hindrance to productivity. If you have one item on your desk, you have a single focus. If you have five items, your focus will be divided in five directions. If you have piles of papers from various projects, different to-do lists, random post-it notes and miscellaneous gadgets and junk, your attention is divided by twenty times or more.

Let me ask . . . What will make you more effective and productive: being focused on one thing or being pulled in a dozen directions?

1. Start by clearing everything off the top of your desk and any tables attached to your desk. Put it all into one of the boxes. Open your desk drawers and empty them into the box. Put everything in the box; pictures, pens, staplers, books, loose paper, knick-knacks—everything that isn't attached.

2. Now take the top item out of the box. Prepare to move fast. Get in the mindset of "How much can I get rid of?" Ban from your mind the "just in case" syndrome. "I'll keep this just in case I need it later." Don't let that fool you, be strong and have no mercy as you go through your clutter. Clutter will slow you down.

Take up one item at a time and ask these questions:

- Do I really need it?

- Can I throw it away?

- Have I looked at it in the last three months?

Be ruthless with yourself and get rid of stuff that you'll never use, look at, or read.

Throw it away, now!

If yes, you do need to keep it, find a place to put it other than on the top of your desk. A stapler could be kept in a drawer or on a shelf. Put things in your drawers that you'll use frequently (rubber bands, pens, pencils, etc.). Don't store it on the desktop; only have it there if you're currently using it. Put it in its new permanent storage place.

If it's paper or something you need to take action on, stack it on your desk. You'll go through that stack in a little bit.

Concerning your desk drawers

You have permission to save one drawer to throw stuff you're not sure what to do with into. But you will be purging that drawer every 30 to 45 days. Put that in your calendar right now: "purge my desk" I'm waiting . . . Did you put it in your calendar?

You should have a file drawer where you keep only files.

Your other drawers should be for your stapler, labeler, rubber bands, pencils, pens, and other tools of the trade that you use several times a week. Do not clutter your drawers with unused junk that you might, hope to, perhaps, or maybe will try to use.

Deal with the paper items in and around your desk

You'll need your catchall list and your working list on your desk.

You will also need to have a day or week planner of some type.

Pick up a piece of paper. What do you need to do with it? Can you throw it away? Most of your papers will fall into this category. Make quick decisions and toss things as much as possible.

A. Is there an action to take? Write it on your working list, catchall list, or calendar.

For example:

> *Pay insurance* goes on the working list or in the calendar.

> *Call Judy about cost report* goes on the working list.

> *Plan vacation with wife* goes on the personal catchall list.

Now look again at the paper that provoked you to write it on a list or in your day planner. Do you need to save that paper or can you throw it away? If it needs to be saved put it in a separate "to file" pile on the edge of your clean desk. We'll get to that pile in a little bit.

B. Is the action time-sensitive? Does it need to be done on a certain day, week or month? If yes, write that action down in your day planner on the appropriate date. Throw the paper away or put it in the "to file" pile.

C. Before you can take an action, does someone else need to provide information or finish a step in the process? You could write this in your calendar so you remember to follow up on a certain day with that person.

Now throw the paper away or put it in the "to file" pile if you need to save it.

If you followed these steps you should have a clean desk and workspace, a list of actions to take, and a pile of papers you need to file. And yes, you'll also have a full bag of trash.

Doesn't it feel good to have gotten rid of excess stuff and be looking at an organized list of things you need to get done? You should feel a big weight off your shoulders.

You can follow this same procedure with clearing the clutter from filing cabinets, closets, the garage, or any room at home.

"Don't agonize. Organize." — *Florence Kennedy*

FILING THE PAPERS THAT NEED TO BE SAVED

There should be a drawer in your desk made to hold file folders. You're going to set this up to hold papers and information that you need access to on a regular basis. Other files will go in a two—or four-drawer file cabinet away from your desk.

Take out your blank file folders. I write the file names with a pencil, but you can use a pen or labeler if you want. I find a pencil to be fast, efficient, and easy to correct.

I prefer to put my three-tabbed files in a larger accordion style of file, one that can hold seven or eight separate files. This keeps them from tipping over in the drawer and makes it easy to grab them out when I need to.

I will use my workload as an example of what you can do with the files.

I have a file folder named "follow up painting calls." I put in there the customers I need to call within the next two weeks. Once I've made the calls, I file them away in the bigger filing cabinet.

Make files that match areas of your life that you deal with on a regular basis.

I have files for current projects labeled: "Book writing," "Current Advertising for Painting," and files with the names of current coaching clients I'm working with.

You will need files that match your current projects.

You should have a "reading" file for articles and papers you need to read but can't get to right away. You can put an article or report in that file folder and make a note on one of your working lists to remind you to read it.

You can also write on a piece of paper a book you want to read and put it in that file for a reminder. You might be at a conference and someone will mention a book that had an impact on them. Make a note of the book title and author and put that note in the "reading file" folder.

Have files connected with what's on your working list. This enables you to keep all the information you need to take the proper action in one easily accessible place. It's okay to have one piece of paper in a file folder. The folders are for you to have easy and fast access to the information you need for your current projects. Do what works best for you.

Time to go through your "to file pile"

Now it's time to deal with the pile of papers on your desk. Take the top piece of paper and decide what to do with it. What action needs to be taken?

If nothing needs to be done, throw it away.

If it's a phone call to make, write that on your working list with the name and phone number of the person to call.

If it's a time-sensitive phone call, write it in your calendar on the appropriate day. Now you can throw away that piece of paper.

But suppose the paper contains important information that you need when you make the call. You can do a couple of different things.

One is having a file folder marked "Phone Calls" you can slip it in there. Or you can have a file with the person's name you need to call and file it there. Just put it where you know you'll find it.

Keep going through the "to file pile" one paper at a time. Force yourself to make a decision. If there is an action to take, write it on the working list and then either throw the paper away or file it.

Don't hesitate to put only one piece of paper in one file folder. The purpose is to be so organized that you can quickly access whatever information you need when you need it.

Sometimes I will use two file folders for the same item and cross-reference them.

I have a folder named "Health Exercises" and a folder named "Exercises."

I wasn't sure where to file my articles on different exercise routines. So I put the article in the "Health Exercises" file and then wrote on a sheet of paper, "see health exercise folder" and put that in the exercise folder. Now I know I have all my bases covered.

Keep your inbox empty

As papers come in each day, put them in your inbox. Your goal is to have an empty inbox at the end of the day. Only put in your inbox the things that come in that day. At the end of the day, empty your inbox by doing one of four things; throw away, put on action list, act on immediately, or file.

Reoccurring tasks

If you have reoccurring tasks that need to be done use your day planner to remember these. I'll make a note at the beginning of each month when bills need to be paid. Once I pay a bill in June, I will immediately make a note on the appropriate day in July so I remember to pay that reoccurring bill.

CLEAR YOUR DESK AND WORKSPACE

Right now, write a reminder to purge and clean your desk again in two months. When you see that note in two months, reorganize your desk, then make a note for two months down the line from that date.

Write in your planner to clean your car every two weeks.

Make a note in your calendar for date nights with your spouse.

At the beginning of the year, write the birthdays of family members and friends you want to remember.

Don't trust your memory. You don't want to use up your brainpower trying to remember appointments, anniversaries or birthdays, etc.

Write everything down and save your brainpower for being creative and coming up with all those great ideas. Now it's time to enjoy your clean desk.

"Time you enjoy wasting is not wasted time."

~*Marthe Troly-Curtin*

12

RELEASE AND RELAX CHOOSING TO WASTE TIME IS A TIME SAVER

Releasing expectations

Some may say there is nothing wrong with expectations, but I disagree. The emotional and spiritual atmosphere around expectations stirs up feelings of "have to" rather than "want to."

When a spouse expects their partner to perform in a certain way, they feel the pressure of that expectation and feel that they have to measure up to that expectation or they will be a disappointment.

When we go to work because it's expected, we will dread waking up and facing the workweek.

When we do volunteer work because we think others expect us to, we labor under a heavy weight.

There is no joy in having to do something, but there is joy in wanting to do something.

How should we handle expectations? After all, I do need to go to work in order to pay my bills and eat.

There are two kinds of expectations, the real ones and the false ones.

False expectations are abound, while real expectations are few. Both are dangerous and you handle them differently. False expectations you get rid of as fast as possible; real expectations you change from "have tos" into "want tos."

False expectations are burdens you put on yourself or burdens others put on you, but they are not burdens God has put on you.

God's calling for our lives—His commandments and His work—are not burdens.

Jesus said, *"Come to me all who labor and are under heavy burdens and I will give you rest. For my yoke is easy and my burden is light."* (Matthew 11:28,30)

John the Apostle clearly spoke to us when he said,

"For this is the love of God, that we keep His commandments. And His commandments are not burdensome." (1 John 5:3)

When God calls us to something, it is not a burden or wearisome. What God calls us to He helps us carry. If you find yourself consistently burned out and weighed down then you're not doing the work of God because his work is restful. (Notice I said consistently.)

False expectations can come from the fear of man or an unhealthy desire to please someone. We say yes to tasks and projects because we fear someone's disapproval or we want to impress someone.

False expectations come from comparing ourselves to others. God made each of us unique, with unique strengths and unique weaknesses. When you say, "I should be doing this," or "I should be doing that," that is not wise. *Embrace who you are; learn from others but don't try to be them.* (2 Corinthians 10:12)

Therefore, the best thing to do with false expectations is to cut them loose as soon as possible. Then be still and hear God's small voice telling you what to do and which way to go.

Real expectations are things like going to work and being faithful and true in relationships. However, you don't want those to be "have tos."

Here is how you change "have tos" into "want tos".

Change the way you approach things. In the letter to the Thessalonians Paul says, "*In everything give thanks for this is the will of God in Christ Jesus for you.*" (1 Thessalonians 5:18)

You can, as an act of faith, approach every situation with a grateful heart. You commit to verbally expressing thanks for your job or spouse or children. When you release thanks through your mouth, it begins to take root in your heart.

You don't have to feel thankful to be thankful, but when you choose to be thankful, you will begin to feel thankful.

Walk by faith not feelings and your feelings will begin to follow your faith.

In those areas of your life that you're feeling expectations, such as work or with a spouse, and it's robbing you of joy in that area, then make a list of the thing you appreciate about the situation or person.

What is it about work that you can be thankful for? Instead of complaining about the long commute be thankful that it gives you time to listen to learning tapes or Bible CDs.

Over an average year, you could gain 490 hours of instruction in an area you want to improve.

With a spouse, make a list of all the things you appreciate about them. We too often focus on the little irritations and can become embittered.

However, if you make a list of the things that are pure, good, and lovely about your spouse, then focus on those things and express thanks to God and your spouse about those things, amazing things will happen in your own heart and in the lives of those you are thankful for.

Rest

Everyone needs a break. Without rest and renewal you'll find yourself being redundant in your activities and thus wasting a lot of time.

You need to step away from your work on a regular basis to be recharged. There's a physical, emotional and spiritual reason why God said to rest one day a week. No work calls, no emails, no work.

Learn how to waste time with forethought

Putting in long workdays on a regular basis is also a waste of time. You need to stop and rest each day where you can put your pressures behind you.

Also, throughout your workday take breaks. Work for 50 minutes then get up, stretch, do some simple exercises, take a short walk, relax and then get back to your focused work.

Leisure time is as valuable as work time for long-term success.

Find a leisure time activity that you could do: Ballroom dancing, cooking, painting, pottery, or gardening, etc.

You need to find time daily, weekly and monthly for leisure and rest with no work allowed. This will make you more productive.

> *"Besides the noble art of getting things done,*
> *there is the noble art of leaving things undone.*

The wisdom of life consists in the elimination of non-essentials." Lin Yutang, The Importance Of Living.

13

REVIEW

1. Gather: Get everything out of your mind and onto paper.

2. Prioritize: Make the decision of what is most important to work on first. Sort and organize the list you made of all your thoughts, dreams, projects, and concerns.

3. Plan: Be diligent to plan out your projects step by step, beginning with the end in mind. Plan your month, week and day.

5. Focused action: Stay focused on your plan. Don't take on too much. Do not multi-task!

6. Act: Take massive action on what you've planned. Move quickly, act fast.

7. Release: Put aside perfectionism and expectations. Enter into the works God has prepared for you and you'll find peace and rest.

8. Relax: Work hard but learn how to relax and do nothing. Even God rested on the seventh day. Reward yourself daily for a job well done.

    Work hard when it's time to work, play with enthusiasm when it's time to play, and relax peacefully when it's time to put your feet up.

9. Daily you'll be adding to your catchall list, calendar and working list. These are the foundations of your system. Don't trust your memory—use your lists.

"Life is full of ups and downs, so put your hands in the air and enjoy the ride."

~Unknown

14

HELPFUL ADVICE TO KEEP YOU ON TRACK

Life is an adventure. Planning is good, and it will help you avoid many difficulties and problems. However, a good plan will not prevent all the hassles and interruptions life throws at you.

You will get knocked off course. Here are some helpful tips and reminders that will get you back on the road of productivity again

"No is a complete sentence and so often we forget that. When we don't want to do something we can simply smile and say no. We don't have to explain ourselves, we can just say No."

~Susan Gregg

15

SAYING NO

The single most powerful time management tool is the ability to say no.

Time cannot be managed; it's like a river that keeps flowing no matter what you do with it. We jump into the river of time with our tasks and projects.

We can only carve out of each day time to do the things we choose to do. We can manage our tasks, projects, dreams, thinking, skills, weaknesses and goals, but we cannot move time, add time or rearrange time. We can move tasks, add tasks and rearrange tasks, but time remains constant.

When you say yes to one thing you're saying no to another. If you say yes to sleeping in, you're saying no to extra time for personal growth.

When you say yes to working long hours you're saying to your wife, "I don't want to spend this time with you."

When you say yes to mowing the lawn you're saying no to writing that report that could make you $1000.

You must make sure that whatever you say yes to is worth the price of saying no to something else.

Don't bite off more than you can chew. Be honest with people (and yourself) about what you can take on and they will respect you for it. Use time wisely. Schedule your day. Know what needs to be done and the time it takes to do it. Prioritize on importance and need. Delegate. If you can't fit something into your schedule, no matter how tempting, don't accept it! Don't be a "YES man." Just say NO!

Stress is created when you take on too many projects and tasks. Stress causes you to work inefficiently and slows you down, thus taking even more time to get something done, which puts more stress on you.

It's easier and healthier just to say no.

When you give yourself permission to stop doing things you'll feel a heavy weight lift off your shoulders.

The question isn't how can I get more done? The question is what can I stop doing?

Use your future, maybe-do list and folder. Here is where you dump all your ideas and potential projects. It is a holding tank that will free your mind to focus on the projects that you really want to do and need to do now.

What can I stop doing?

You can stop doing the projects you took on because of a false sense of obligation.

You can stop the programs you became a part of to impress someone else.

You can stop doing the project you took on because it was the "responsible" thing to do. In other words it was a guilt trip.

Go ahead and make your list of the things you need to stop doing. (Even if it hurts your mom's feelings)

Control your projects and you control how your time is used. Control your projects or they will control you.

How to say no

Saying no will garner people's respect and drive away those you don't want to deal with anyway. People respect you when you have boundaries and are not a pushover.

Saying no will give you more time to do the things you want to do and the things you're good at doing, that will increase your productivity and quality of work. By saying no you decrease the pressures and stress in your life.

You can learn to say no in a polite and kind way.

You can start out by thanking the person who asked you for considering you, and thank them for their concern about the project they want you to get involved in. Then let them know about your time limitations, how you've already made other commitments, and how will not be able to help at this time.

If someone from church approaches you and asks you to be involved in the upcoming spring festival, you can say, "Thank you for considering me. I've always been blessed by that event, but at this time I have other commitments that would keep me from giving it the attention it deserves."

Other ways of saying no:

> "I'm sorry I can't. I don't have the time to do a good job at it."

> "That sounds like it could be a great idea, but it's not a fit for me right now."

> "No, I can't do that."

> "I can't do this, I have other commitments."

> "I don't think I'm the best person for this. Why don't you ask . . . ?"

Keep your answer simple. Don't over-talk trying to explain all the reasons why you can't take something on.

Remember, you don't have to respond immediately. Just say, "Let me think about that and I'll get back to you." If a person presses for an immediate answer I always say, "If you want an answer now the answer is no, but if you give me some time to think about it, then I might be able to do something."

Learn to say no to answering your phone whenever it rings. There is no law that commands you to answer the phone when it rings.

"Procrastination is the thief of time, collar him."

~Charles Dickens, David Copperfield

16

ENDING PROCRASTINATION (EVENTUALLY)

Procrastination is costly, and one of its biggest costs is the effect it has on our mind and emotions. Procrastination burdens us with guilt and makes us feel bad about the kind of person we are. Procrastination consumes major portions of our mind and thoughts.

When we keep putting things off, we waste time and we waste creative energy by spending too much time in worry and regret.

When you procrastinate and don't get that card for a family member's birthday or miss the due date on your electric bill, you are weighed down with guilt and regret. These emotions start a chain reaction that robs us of the energy we need to get other tasks done. We feel discouraged over our failure to take action so we take even less action.

ENDING PROCRASTINATION (EVENTUALLY)

Every time we procrastinate, we put a burden on our mental and emotional shoulders that weighs upon us and slows us down.

We procrastinate for different reasons:

1. We are afraid of failing, so we keep putting it off.

2. We just don't like doing that kind of task.

3. We don't want to make a decision because we're afraid of making people unhappy with us.

4. We fear success, so we don't even start.

5. We are overwhelmed; we have too much on our plate. Picture a large ocean wave coming at you; it towers above you and smashes you into the sand, rolling you over and over. That is what overwhelm is like. All your tasks and responsibilities hit you, knocking you off your feet and creating inaction.

Why do you procrastinate? Stop right now and think about the answer to that question. It's worth your time to honestly examine your reasons. Knowledge is the first step to change.

Have you ever finished a project quickly without procrastination? Why were you able to do that? What was different about that project?

The hardest part in most chores or projects is the first step.

Conquering procrastination—a little pain now or greater pain later.

We choose procrastination because it accomplishes two things: It gives us momentary pleasure and distracts us from pain.

The pain is the difficult task before us: the phone call you don't want to make, the paper you need to write, the person who needs confronting, the backlog that needs to be filed.

Distractions, like Facebook, surfing the web, reading, or socializing, temporarily remove the pain of doing the work.

What you need to do is paint a picture of the pain you will suffer if you don't focus on your task now.

Then paint a picture of how you'll feel when you finish this task. Use your imagination and emotion.

Basic Tips for Stopping Procrastination

Here are some mind tricks to overcome inertia:

1. Use deadlines.

   Set a deadline when you will have chapter one done by. Ask a friend to hold you accountable to a certain date for finishing your marketing plan. Set a firm "I will call 10 new prospects" by this date.

Deadlines, even arbitrary ones, can get you moving but you need to put the deadline in your calendar with some reminders along the way.

The "shiny penny" syndrome is a big waster of time. We can be so busy trying to find the next best tool to use that we don't use anything. We spend our time researching instead of working.

Put a time limit on your research; set a timer.

2. Break up big projects into small five to 10 minute tasks.

    Take really small steps. If you need to make a difficult phone call then take the step of looking up the number.

3. Stop and think about what it is you really want to accomplish.

    Say to yourself, "I don't want to do this, but why do I need to get this done? What is the deeper purpose?" Refocusing on the reason and purpose generates motivation.

4. Take time to play, and give yourself permission to have fun.

    Set up some regular times where you disconnect from work and unwind, have fun, explore and relax, doing only that which you want to do. When we are under stress, we tend to procrastinate more, but play relieves stress. Work and play are equally important as they both make you productive.

5. Since overwhelm causes procrastination, get rid of some of the items on your to-do list. Pass them on to someone else or simply scratch them off your list. Do you really need to do that?

6. Exercise. Get up off your chair and do some simple exercises for four minutes.

   Get your heart rate up and your metabolism burning. You'll be surprised at how this will motivate you to get back to work and tackle that hard task you were putting off.

7. Reward yourself.

   Set a timer for 15, 20 or 30 minutes and tell yourself that if you work straight through until the timer goes off you can read your novel for 10 minutes, or go get your favorite snack or watch your favorite movie.

8. Organize your desk.

   Clutter is confusing and can shut down our mind. Take five minutes to clear your desk and organize your papers. Now you're ready to tackle the job before you. Sometimes organizing a closet or your bedroom can have the same effect as it releases certain roadblocks in our mind and frees up our mental processes to get back and focus on the work we've been putting off. I don't know why this works but I've seen it help different people.

9. Try saying to yourself, "I don't have to do this but I want to get it done and off my mind." Or "I don't have to do the whole thing right now but I can do this one simple step."

10. Do the hardest thing first, just get it out of the way and put it behind you. Give yourself a reward when you're finished.

11. Or do the easiest thing first. Sometimes all you need to do is get the ball rolling. Start with the easiest action and see if it gets your productive juices flowing.

"Feed your faith and your fears will starve to death."

~Author Unknown

17

OVERCOMING WORRY AND FEAR

Worry accomplishes nothing. It never has and it never will. It only consumes your brainpower with "what ifs" and "what might be's". This will only cause discomfort and keep you from reaching your goals.

What you focus on will grow. Many people live mainly from their fears because they feed their fears. They feed their fears by focusing on their fears. The opposite of fear is faith. You need to feed your faith, not your fear.

One of the biggest time wasters is worrying. Worry focuses on what you don't want instead of focusing on what you do want.

When fear strikes, you escape by doing useless tasks, surfing the Internet, checking your email 10 times a day, getting on Facebook, and hanging out at the water cooler.

Worry is the dread of what might happen. You begin focusing on what might be and it gives you anxiety and even affects your body. Your heart rate changes, and your stomach begins to turn and twist.

Regret is the evil twin of worry. Regret looks back at things that you can't change. It's time to put the past to rest and move on.

Forgive yourself, forgive others and move into today.

How to handle fear and worry

You handle fear by facing it directly and asking some questions. Let's say you fear losing your job.

Ask yourself these questions:

"What steps could I take to make my job more secure?"

Perhaps I could go directly to my boss and ask what I can do to improve my performance. I could also read and study to improve the skills I need to advance in my line of work.

"What's the worst thing that could happen if I lost my job?"

I would miss my house payments and have to live on the streets. Then I would move in with a relative. I would lose my car because of missed payments. I would have no income, therefore, I could buy no food so I'd starve and die. Taking things to the extreme can often break the cycle of worry.

"What are the positive things that could come from losing my job?"

I would have some time off to relax and do some things I've never had time for before. I may finally escape the job I never really liked and find the ideal job I've always wanted.

"If I were fired, what would be my plan for the next four months?"

I could take a week to get away, regroup, and evaluate my life, dreams, and passions. I could come up with an exciting resume, do some research on the ideal job I want and get creative on how to approach potential employers. The process of dreaming and planning will change your focus from your fears to your possibilities.

Face your fears and they will begin to melt into the shadows.

> *"Confront your fears, list them, get to know them, and only then will you be able to put them aside and move ahead."*—Jerry Gille

Words from the past: "It's a clever idea,
Mr. Bell, but don't wire us, we'll wire you."

~Robert Brault

18

TELEPHONE

The telephone along with its electronic cousins is a great time waster. With their bells, whistles and various sounds they demand your attention at inopportune times.

Pick times throughout the day when you turn off your phone, close your Internet windows and turn off your email notifications. Let people know when you'll be available by phone and let them know what times of the day you return calls.

You don't have to answer all your calls and you don't have to be reachable all the time.

I used to have a very competent worker who would call me several times a day wondering about certain work situations he would encounter. He was insecure about making a wrong decision so he would call me for every little thing that came up. I started to ignore the phone when I saw his number. I felt that if I forced him to make decisions on his own he would stop being dependent. It worked; he was forced to make decisions on the job site because he couldn't reach me. Eventually he stopped calling, and in all the years he worked for me, he never made a bad decision.

Let most of your calls go to voicemail. If I'm really wanting to answer a call from a customer, I will save their number in my cell phone contacts. I will type it in "cust", then their name, and the date. So it will look like this—Cust Fred 4-12-13. Now when they call I will see their name and know to answer.

Plan your phone calls

Before you get on the phone know what you want to say, why you are making the call, and what you hope the outcome of the call will be.

This will help you stay focused and you'll get to your point quickly and off the phone fast.

If someone calls you and rambles, then let them know you have to get to another appointment, project or whatever they pulled you away from. Ask them specifically; what can I do for you?

You can also ask them to put their question or request in writing via email so you can give it the time it deserves. This is reserved for talkers that have a hard time getting to their point. But if you can get them to briefly state their question or issue so you can respond quickly, then that is the preferred choice.

Stop phone tag

Leave a message that tells them when the best time to call you back is.

Be detailed in what you want from them and ask them to leave it on your voice mail or send it via email.

Ask them to tell you when the best time to return their call is.

"If the only way you could read an email was to run a mile first, the urge would quickly die. Human beings constantly do subconscious effort/reward calculations. Tapping a screen is the easiest of physical tasks."

~ Andrew Weil

19

EMAIL TIPS

Use an email signature letting people know you only answer your email once a day or once every three days. This way they won't be expecting an immediate answer.

Don't look at email before 11am or after 4 pm (or whatever time suits you best). The point is to break your addiction to checking email every 10 to 15 minutes.

Start unsubscribing from junk email.

Learn how to use your email filters so only the important emails land in your inbox.

Use Sanebox to help filter and control your email.

Use canned responses for common questions.

Keep your inbox clear by deleting, responding or filing.

"The average American worker has fifty interruptions a day, of which seventy percent have nothing to do with work."

~ W. Edwards Deming

20

INTERRUPTIONS

Don't allow interruptions. You can control 80% of interruptions.

1. Go to a location away from others so you can concentrate.

2. Turn off phones, email, and other items that will pull your mind in different directions.

3. Let others know when you need time without any questions or interruptions.

4. Start work earlier. Develop the habit of getting up before anyone else. By rising 60 minutes earlier, you can find a lot of uninterrupted time.

5. Or, if you're a night owl, stay up a couple of hours later than normal. You can find some peace and quiet late at night after everyone else is asleep.

6. If you have to visit someone go to his or her office. This gives you the freedom to leave when you want. If they're in your office you have to ask them to leave and that can be awkward. Alternatively you can meet at a neutral place.

"While one person hesitates because he feels inferior, the other is busy making mistakes and becoming superior."

~ Henry C. Link

21

TAKING THE FIRST STEP

The hardest part of any task is getting started. Take exercising for example. Once you start it's easy to keep going, but the starting is the hard part.

You think about starting, you plan to start, but you don't get started.

If you can cross that invisible line of taking action things can get going rather quickly. The best way to take action is to not think about it. The best way to not think about it is to plan ahead.

You get your motivation during the planning. Make your decisions when you plan so when it's time to act, you don't have to decide; it's already been decided. You act; don't think.

Don't second-guess your planning and decisions when it's time to act. Turn off that part of the brain and just move.

Too often this is what happens. The alarm goes off, you're half-awake, and you roll to your side and push yourself up to a sitting position, stare at the floor, stand up and stagger into the bathroom. Yesterday you had planned to start exercising regularly, you were motivated to get in shape, lose that tummy fat and develop those six-pack abs. But now, leaning against the bathroom sink and staring into the mirror, you begin second-guessing your decision.

Stop, don't think, just act.

> *"If you spend too much time thinking about a thing, you'll never get it done."*—Bruce Lee

Don't argue with yourself. The decision has already been made, so don't second-guess your decision. Just start exercising and once you start it will be easy to keep going.

You planned ahead about writing four times a week. The best time to write is at 6:30 am to 9:00 am. You enjoy writing but it's hard to get started.

6:30 rolls around, you're sitting at your desk but now the procrastinator tries to take over. You see an area in your office that needs organizing or you get curious—Did I answer the email from Tom? Or you see a program on your computer that you wanted to check out and before you realize it two hours have passed by and you have not done any writing.

What should you do? Stick with your plan. You've already decided. Don't think, just act.

Act during action time, and second-guess during planning time. Schedule regular planning times and do all your thinking at that time. But during action time, there's no more thinking, just go, go, go.

Are you thinking of going on a diet? Sit down and plan a 3-7 day eating plan. This is the time to second-guess, argue with yourself, and make decisions.

But once you've decided you're all set, when mealtime rolls around you don't have to think about what you're going to eat; just act on your already made decisions.

During your planning stage keep things realistic, don't overreach. It's better to end up doing more than what you planned than to keep coming up short. Reaching your pre-set goals and objectives motivates you, so make them low enough to achieve them on a consistent basis and you'll stay motivated.

Make your decisions when you need the least amount of will power. Don't decide to avoid dessert when a plate of brownies is before you. Make that decision beforehand.

When you make your decisions take a minute to picture yourself following through. See yourself saying no to the brownies, see yourself getting right out of bed and exercising, see yourself sitting at your computer ignoring all distractions and writing your book.

Before taking action, get prepared.

Have your exercise clothes laid out ahead of time. If you're using any equipment have it ready to go.

The night before, have your writing material laid out and ready to go.

Have your meals and menu planned and the food purchased so you can prepare it easily.

Make it easy to take action. Have things ready so when your will power is weak you don't need to think, you just act.

"Do the things that need to be done when they need to be done in the way it needs to be done whether you like it or not"—Charles Hobbs Time Power"Whatever failures I have known, whatever errors I have committed, whatever follies I have witnessed in private and public life have been the consequence of action without thought."

~ Bernard M.Baruch on planning

22

YOU NEED TO MAKE A PLAN

Everybody keeps a schedule

You are either keeping a schedule you made for yourself or keeping a schedule that lack of planning is forcing upon you.

Take time to think and plan. Planning saves time, money and energy.

Your schedule is either wasting time or it's making you productive. It all depends on how well you planned.

If you find yourself always running, sprinting from one project to another, feeling harried and harassed, then you have failed to stop and take the time to think.

It's time to stop acting and start thinking.

Usually when we are in this panic state of run, run, run, it is hard to think clearly. All we are doing is reacting, and this kind of reaction is damaging to ourselves, our business, and those around us.

We might have a false sense of importance because we're always busy and always moving. But deep inside we know that we're really getting nowhere fast.

It is time to stop, think and plan. A well thought through plan will enable us to get twice as much done in the same amount of time. And even better, a plan will help us get done what needs to get done and still have time to play, guilt-free!

Take a few minutes every morning to plan, take 30 to 60 minutes each week to plan, and take 3-6 hours each month to plan.

Free Time Management, Productivity Webinar

Sign up for the Free Time Management, Productivity webinar. Jeff will be going over the principles from this book, showing you step by step how to get the ultimate time management system working for you.

Go to: http://biblebasedbusinesses.com/time-management/ and sign up today.

Free Book

"Bible Based Businesses—Biblical Principles for Success in Business and Life." For a limited time you an get this book FREE at **www.Biblebasedbusinesses.com**

ABOUT THE AUTHOR

Jeff Testerman knows how to relate to the business owner. Thirty years ago he started his first business and has gone on to start 12 small businesses in six states. He's done everything from being the sole worker and owner, to having nine employees.

He's the father of 12 children, 9 boys and 3 girls. Four of his children have started their own businesses in Florida, Colorado, and Oregon.

Jeff has learned what it takes to succeed in all areas of life. True success isn't having a big business, it's being balanced in all areas of your life and loving it. It's important that you experience prosperity in all of life, not just business.

Jeff presents, in an organized and easy to understand manner, the principles needed for one to birth, grow, and run their own business.

"He does an excellent job of weaving in his own personal experiences of almost three decades of establishing and running a dozen successful businesses."

Bill Illch

"At the beginning of 2009 I hired Jeff as a business consultant, to help me restructure my businesses. I had been operating for well over a decade with a seriously flawed business structure, but I was not sure what was wrong, or how to fix it.

In two days, Jeff was able to analyze, plan and enact an array of changes, which dramatically improved my businesses. I recouped my investment in his services within two weeks, and found myself wishing I had sought his advice years earlier.

I was very impressed with Jeff's ability to come in and, from a cold start, see through my defective jumble of procedures and priorities, and discern exactly what was needed to turn things around from failure to success.

In hindsight, I can see that I would have faced serious business collapse and damaging losses within a few months, if I had not retained Jeff when I did.

As a side note, the improvement to my marriage, resulting from my decision to retain Jeff as a business consultant, would alone make my investment in his services overwhelmingly worthwhile.

I strongly recommend Jeff's training and consultation services to anyone in business. He has the insight and acumen to turn your enterprise into a faithful and profitable servant for you, which will surely bless your home and family."

Stan Avery, Owner, Avery Services, LLC, dba Avery Plumbing and Director, Unreached Villages, Inc.

Check out my blogs at:

www.BibleBasedBusinesses.com

www.JeffTesterman.com

You can contact Jeff Testerman at
Dadof12@gmail.com

31833307R00078

Made in the USA
Charleston, SC
29 July 2014